RUGBY TO BIRMINGHAM

Vic Mitchell and Keith Smith

Vic Mitchell

10/2008

 Middleton Press

Front cover: Daventry was the setting for this fine record of a typical local train, southbound on 6th September 1958. No. 41285 was a 2-6-2T of LMS origin. (G.Adams/M.J.Stretton coll.)

Back cover: No. 86245 Caledonian *propels an express bound for Euston out of Birmingham International on 26th March 2002. (P.Jones)*

Published October 2008

ISBN 978 1 906008 37 6

© *Middleton Press, 2008*

Design Deborah Esher

Typesetting Barbara Mitchell

Published by
> *Middleton Press*
> *Easebourne Lane*
> *Midhurst*
> *West Sussex*
> *GU29 9AZ*

Tel: 01730 813169
Fax: 01730 812601
Email: info@middletonpress.co.uk
www.middletonpress.co.uk

Printed & bound by Biddles Ltd, Kings Lynn

CONTENTS

INDEX

ACKNOWLEDGEMENTS

We are very grateful for the assistance received from many of those mentioned in the credits also to B.Bennett, A.R.Carder, L.Crosier, G.Croughton, F.Hornby, S.C.Jenkins, N.Langridge, B.Lewis, J.P.McCrickard, Mr D. and Dr S.Salter, M.Turvey, T.Walsh, E.Wilmshurst and in particular, our always supportive wives, Barbara Mitchell and Janet Smith.

I. Railway Clearing House map for 1947, with later additions.

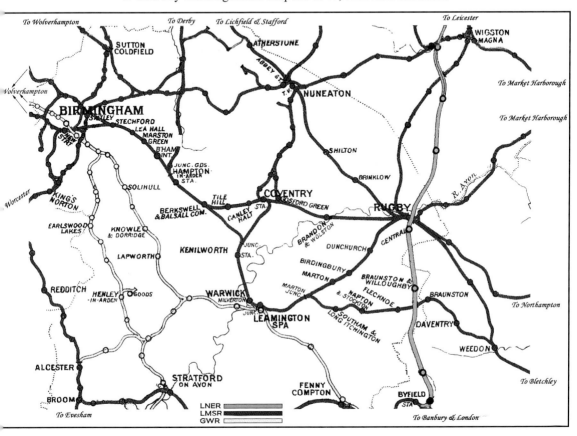

GEOGRAPHICAL SETTING

Our journey starts at the historic town of Rugby, which is situated on a Limestone outcrop, which gave rise to cement production. The River Avon flows west, north of the town, and curves southwards, south of Coventry, to reach Leamington Spa. The main line descends from Rugby to pass over the river on its approach to Coventry and then climbs over an area of mudstones to pass through a ridge, in Beechwood Tunnel.

A second descent follows to the valley of the north flowing River Blyth at Hampton-in-Arden and a final climb ensues to reach the commercial complex of Birmingham. The entire line was built within the county of Warwickshire, but its boundary has changed in recent years.

The route west from Weedon traversed Lower Lias (limestone and clay) and it joined the line from Rugby on its approach to the valley of the River Leam. The Avon and Leam meet west of the spa town centre. The Weedon-Braunston section was in Northamptonshire, but the remainder was in Warwickshire.

The maps are to the scale of 25ins to 1 mile, with north at the top, unless otherwise indicated.

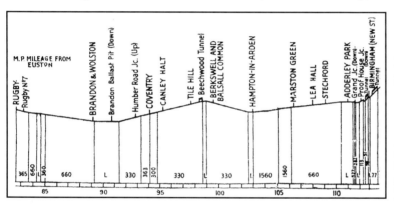

II. Main line gradient profile.

III. 1946 map at 4 miles to 1ins. Rugby is in the centre and Weedon is lower right.

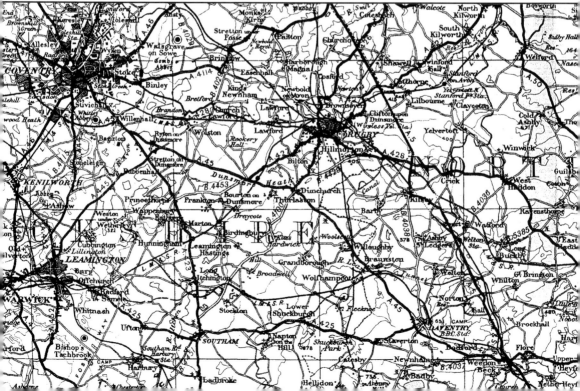

HISTORICAL BACKGROUND

The Act for the London & Birmingham Railway was passed on 6th May 1833 and the line from London to Birmingham (Curzon Street) was completed on 9th April 1838, although buses were provided for the 35 miles south of Rugby until 24th June 1838. The Grand Junction Railway linked Curzon Street with the 1830 Liverpool & Manchester Railway from 1837. All trains used this terminus until New Street was completed in 1854. The LBR opened a branch from Coventry to Leamington Spa (Milverton) on 9th December 1844.

Running north from Hampton-in-Arden from 1839 was the Birmingham & Derby Junction Railway. This company ran into Birmingham (Lawley Street) from 1842 and became part of the Midland Railway in 1844. The Midland Counties Railway ran north from Rugby to Leicester from 1840 and was also a constituent of the MR from 1844. The GJR and LBR became part of the London & North Western Railway when it was formed on 16th July 1846.

The LNWR opened the Trent Valley route between Rugby and Stafford in 1847, this enabling long distance trains to bypass Birmingham. It completed the Coventry-Nuneaton link in 1850.

The Great Western Railway opened its Didcot & Chester Line through Leamington (Spa) in 1852, but the LNWR had reached that town from Rugby in February 1851. The link between that route at Marton Junction and the London line at Weedon was completed on 1st August 1895 by the LNWR, although the section east of Daventry had come into use earlier, on 1st March 1888.

The LNWR provided a link between Kenilworth and Berkswell in 1884 mostly for use by freight trains. (It had only one regular passenger train by 1953 and closed completely in 1969.) There was a goods line (Coventry Loop or Avoiding Line) through the eastern suburbs of Coventry from Humber Road Junction to Three Spires Junction between 1914 and 1984, although the southern half mile closed in 1963.

The LNWR became a constituent of the London Midland & Scottish Railway in 1923. Its area formed the London Midland Region of British Railways upon nationalisation in 1948.

The name "North London Railways" was applied from 31st March 1994 to the services to Birmingham via Northampton. These were renamed Silverlink Trains after privatisation on 29th September 1997, when a 7½ year franchise was taken by the National Express Group. Virgin West Coast Trains took over main line operations, with the exception of ScotRail sleeper services, on a 15 year franchise. Central Trains operated over the route from Rugby to Birmingham, also serving the Midlands and way beyond.

London Midland came into being on 11th November 2007 and it took over all services in our area, except Virgin ones.

Closures
Passenger services to Leamington Spa were withdrawn from:

> Weedon 15th September 1958
> Rugby 15th June 1959
> Nuneaton 18th January 1965
> (via Kenilworth also from Berkswell)

Freight withdrawal dates are given in the captions.

Electrification

25th October 1965:	Rugby - Coventry catenary energised.
3rd January 1966:	Rugby - Coventry electrified passenger and freight services commenced.
15th August 1966:	Coventry - Stechford - Aston - Bescot catenary energised.
3rd October 1966:	Coventry - Bescot (via Aston) electrified freight services commenced.
31st October 1966:	Stechford - Birmingham New Street - Wolverhampton catenary energised.
5th December 1966:	Coventry - Birmingham - Wolverhampton and Birmingham - Walsall electrified services commenced.
2nd January 1967:	Rugby - Birmingham - Wolverhampton existing services worked electrically.
6th March 1967:	Rugby - Birmingham - Wolverhampton full electrified timetable commenced.

PASSENGER SERVICES

Rugby to Leamington Spa

There were five trains, weekdays only, in 1851, the figure increasing to seven by 1871. There were also one or two on Sundays until 1883.

The 1895 timetable showed eight trains through to Warwick (Milverton), two of which omitted four stops. There were still eight, but calling at all stations, in 1921.

Wartime economy meant only six trains in 1945, but this had dropped to five by the end of operation.

Weedon to Leamington Spa

The initial service to Daventry comprised six return trips; by 1895 there were two, plus four more to Leamington, or beyond. These figures still applied in 1920 and 1945, but there was a service withdrawal during part of World War II.

In the final years, there were three through trains, plus one starting west from Napton & Stockton in the early morning.

January 1921

RUGBY, COVENTRY, LEAMINGTON SPA, WARWICK, and BIRMINGHAM.—L. & N. W.
District Supt., J. F. Bradford, Birmingham.

Timetable: Down — Week Days, Week Days (continued), Sat./Sat., Sundays.

Notes:

a Calls at Adderley Park at 10 17 mrn. to set down passengers only.

c Stops by Signal at 6 20 mrn. to take up for beyond Crewe only.

r Runs 5 mins. later on Saturdays.

h Stops at 8 17 aft. to set down from Rugby and the South on informing the Guard.

s Saturdays only.

† New Street Station: about ¼ mile to Moor Street Station (G. W.) and about ⅜ mile to Snow Hill Station (G.W.)

‡ Station for Yardley (1¼ miles).

§ 1¼ miles to Great Western (Coventry Road) Station.

Kenilworth

This town was served by trains from both the aforementioned routes, as well as ones operating between Leamington Spa and Nuneaton, or just Coventry. The frequency was always greater than the routes from the east. The Berkswell Loop carried mainly freight and the few scheduled passenger trains using the cut-off diminished over the years. They were mainly peak-hour trains for local daily-breaders, later known as commuters.

Rugby to Birmingham

The first guide showed four daily trains from London. The figure of ten applied on weekdays in 1850, with four on Sundays. An extra at 7.15am from Rugby on weekdays was the only one to call at all stations on the route.

By 1870, there were six stopping trains, plus eleven fast. On Sundays the figures were three and two respectively. The 1895 timetable offered 20 departures from Rugby on weekdays, with five on Sundays, the stopping pattern being varied.

To chronicle the improvements in the 20th century would produce a mass of generally rising figures, with the exception of the wartime periods.

The advent of electrification brought regular interval services for the first time. London expresses became half-hourly at peak times in May 1969 and throughout the daytime in May 1972. Stopping trains were subject to similar dramatic improvements. Hourly semi-fasts came in May 1972 and stopped at all stations on the route. These became half-hourly and were operated by Network SouthEast upon sectorisation.

The diversion of some Western Region trains via Coventry brought an increase in frequency west thereof, about hourly initially, giving the best service ever.

January 1945

LONDON, RUGBY, COVENTRY, LEAMINGTON SPA, WARWICK, and BIRMINGHAM

1. Rugby to Marton
RUGBY

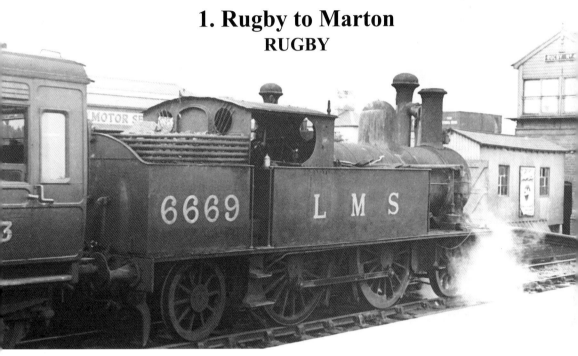

1.   The map can be found with the illustrations and details of the station in pictures 52-59. We start by looking at two locomotives commonly used on the long forgotten rural route to Leamington Spa. Designed by Webb in 1890, this ex-LNWR 2-4-2T is about to depart at 10.5am on 3rd July 1948. (H.C.Casserley)

2.   The elderly 2-4-2Ts gave way to LMS designed 2-6-2Ts of a type introduced in 1946. No. 41285 is heading two coaches on 13th June 1959. It is in north end bay platform No. 6. (P.Kingston)

WEST OF RUGBY

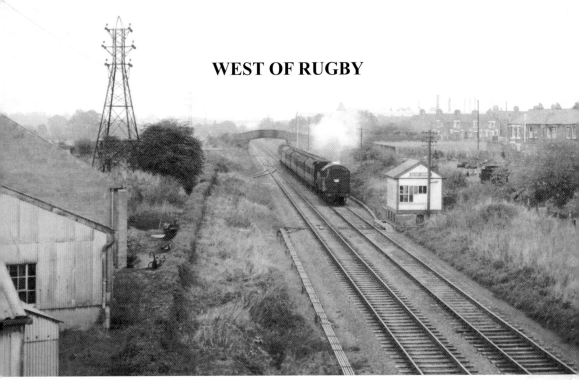

3.   We begin our journey by taking the route south of the cement works. We are one mile from Rugby station and Bilton Siding signal box is seen in 1959. It closed on 26th November 1967. A Rugby to Leamington Spa excursion passes by and it is seen moments later, from the other side of the bridge, in the next picture. The line to Marton Junction was singled in October 1958 and continued to carry coal to Southam Cement Works until 1985. (A.W.V.Mace/Milepost 92 ½)

4.   There was a private siding for the grain silos (right), plus a siding for public goods traffic (left). This was known as New Bilton Wharf and was in use until 25th April 1966. One mile of track to this site existed in 2008 for use by the engineers, but the last traffic was from Redland Tiles in July 1991. The nearby Rugby Cement siding had three or four trains per week bringing in chalk in the early 1960s. (A.W.V.Mace/Milepost 92 ½)

DUNCHURCH

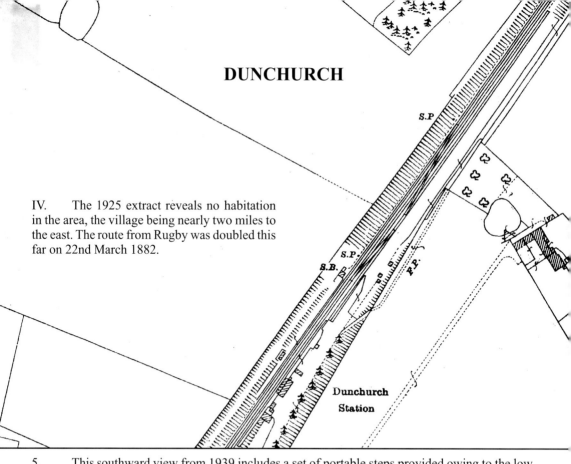

IV.   The 1925 extract reveals no habitation in the area, the village being nearly two miles to the east. The route from Rugby was doubled this far on 22nd March 1882.

Dunchurch
Station

5.   This southward view from 1939 includes a set of portable steps provided owing to the low level of the platform. The station was 4½ miles from Rugby and opened on 1st October 1871. It was north of the A45. (Stations UK)

6.   The local population rose from 920 in 1901 to 1842 in 1961, by which time it was served well by buses. A train from Rugby approaches in the 1950s; the house still served as a dwelling more than 50 years later. (W.A.Camwell/SLS coll.)

7.   A closer view of a train from Rugby, not long before closure to passengers in 1959, features 2-6-2T no. 41228, the cattle dock and the 20-lever signal box, which closed on 1st December 1964. Goods traffic had ceased here one month earlier. (A.W.V.Mace/Milepost 92 ½)

BIRDINGBURY

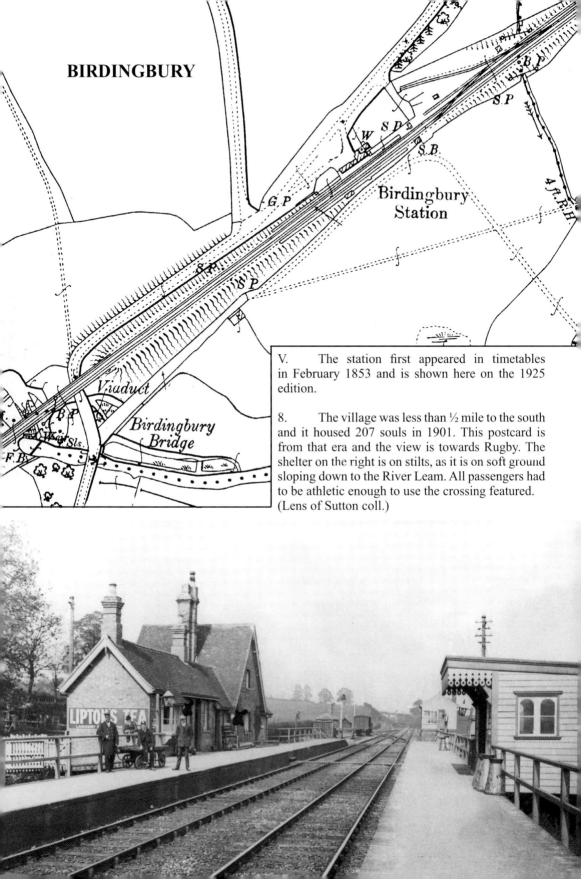

Birdingbury
Station

V.   The station first appeared in timetables
in February 1853 and is shown here on the 1925
edition.

8.   The village was less than ½ mile to the south
and it housed 207 souls in 1901. This postcard is
from that era and the view is towards Rugby. The
shelter on the right is on stilts, as it is on soft ground
sloping down to the River Leam. All passengers had
to be athletic enough to use the crossing featured.
(Lens of Sutton coll.)

9.   No. 41227 propels a Leamington Spa - Rugby service on 2nd May 1959. The evidence of rail joint pumping (left) suggests soft ground and poor maintenance. The paraffin lamp was used to the end. (H.F.Wheeller/R.S.Carpenter coll.)

August 1958

RUGBY and LEAMINGTON SPA

Week Days only

Miles		am		am		am		am	G		pm		non	pm	pm		
	50London (Euston).....dep	..	..	8F30	..	10FA20		10F50	11F20		12 7		12 0	3F45	5K20	..	..
	Rugby (Midland) ....dep	8 13	..	10 24	..	12 12	Saturdays only	12 49	1p19	Saturdays only	2 40	Except Saturdays	2p45	3 35	7 59	..	..
4¼	Dunchurch..................	8 21	..	10 32	..	12 21		12 57	1 27		2 48		2 58	5 43	..	..	..
7	Birdingbury...............	8 26	..	10 37	..	12 26		1 2	1 32		2 53		3 2	5 50	8 14	..	..
8¼	Marton	8 30	..	10 41	..	12 30		1 6	1 36		2 57		3 2	5 56	8 20	..	..
15	Leamington Spa B...{ arr	8 42	..	10 53	..	12 42		1 18	1 48		3 9		3 14	6 8	8 32	..	..
	Leamington Spa B...{ dep	8 47	..	10 55	..	12 44		1 20	1 50		3 11		3 16	6 10	8 34	..	..
15½	Leamington Spa C.....arr	8 49	..	10 57	..	12 46		1 22	1 52		3 13		3 18	6 12	8 36	..	..

Week Days only

Miles		am	T	am		am		pm		pm		pm	pm	V	
	Leamington Spa C..... dep	7 0	7 47	10 32	Saturdays only	1153	Saturdays only	1 0	Wednesdays only	4 30	Except Saturdays	6 20	6 36	7p39	
	Leamington Spa B...{ arr	7 2	7 49	10 34		1155		1 2		4 32		6 22	6 38	7 41	
½	Leamington Spa B...{ dep	7 5	7 53	10 37		1159		1 5	1 40	4 35		6 24	6 44	7 47	
7¼	Marton	7 17	8 5	10 49		1211		17	1 54	4 47		6 37	6 58	7 59	
8½	Birdingbury...............	7 21	8 9	10 53		1215		1 21	1 58	4 51		6 42	7 0	8 3	
11½	Dunchurch..................	7 27	8 15	10 59		1221		1 27		4 57		6 58			
15½	Rugby (Midland) ...... arr	7 37	8 26	11 11		1231		1 38	2 15	5 15			7 15	8 18	
98½	50London (Euston) ..... arr	9FH56	11B78	12FJ48		3F43		4F15	7NL27	4 34				10 49	

A Dep 10 10 am until 28th June and from 6th September	**H** Arr 10 1 am on Saturdays
B Leamington Spa Avenue	**J** Arr 12 58 pm on Saturdays
B Arr 11 5 am on Saturdays	**K** Dep 5 27 pm on Saturdays
C Leamington Spa (Milverton) for Warwick	**L** Restaurant Car from Rugby (Mid.) to London
F Restaurant Car between London (Euston) and Rugby (Midland)	(Euston) except on Saturdays; also except Fridays 13th and 20th June
G Through Train to Coventry arr 2 14 pm (Table 73)	**N** Arr 6 55 pm except on Saturdays commencing 27th June
p pm	
T Through Train Leamington Spa (Milverton) to Northampton (Castle) arr 8 58 am (Table 50)	
V Through Train from Birmingham dep 6 26 pm (Table 75)	
Z Buffet Car between Rugby (Mid.) and London (Euston) except on Saturdays	

10.   Minutes later, the same train passes the site of the goods yard, which had closed on 3rd August 1953. The signal box followed on 15th March 1954; it can be seen in picture no. 8. (H.F.Wheeller/R.S.Carpenter coll.)

11.   The building was photographed in April 1962 and it continues in residential use. The structure on the right was for the benefit of gentlemen. (B.W.L.Brooksbank)

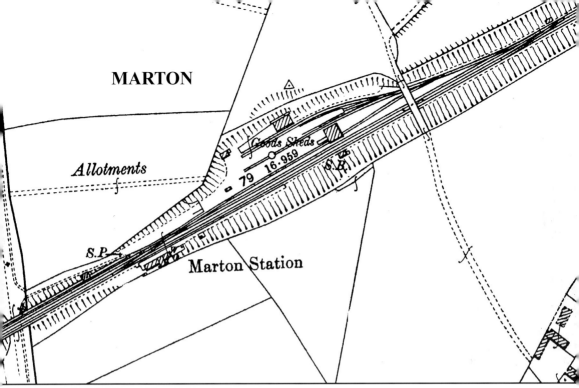

VI.   The station was first shown in timetables from 1st January 1852. The population was 390 in 1901, but the village was nearly one mile to the north. It is seen on the 1905 edition; there had earlier been "Marton Siding" on the up side, ¼ mile northeast of the station and adjacent to the Birdingbury road.

12.   We are now 8¼ miles from Rugby and find staggered platforms with a crossing which is easier to use than the one at Birdingbury. An early postcard includes a notable chimney pot. The track westwards was doubled on 28th January 1884. (Lens of Sutton coll.)

13.   A photograph from 16th August 1947 includes 2-4-2T no. 6683 with the 5.43pm from Rugby to Milverton. Also evident is the signal box, which had 24 levers and functioned until 12th December 1961. (W.A.Camwell/SLS coll.)

14.   The goods yard lasted until 3rd July 1961 and the station building was demolished in 1968. Seen in 1957 is 2-6-2T no. 41227 propelling its train to Rugby towards the bridge which carried a minor lane. Two miles west was Marton Junction, where there was a signal box with 25 levers. It was in use until 4th June 1967. Trains for Southam Cement Works reversed there, but a ground frame sufficed subsequently. The Marton Junction-Leamington Spa section closed for freight on 4th April 1966. (D.K.Jones)

2. Weedon to Kenilworth
WEEDON

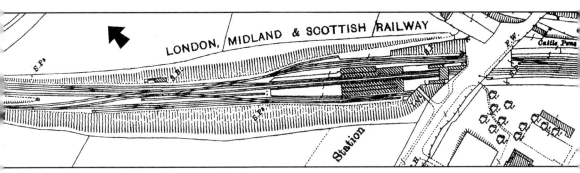

VII.   The 1926 map at 20ins to 1 mile includes only part of the goods yard (right), this closing on 3rd May 1965. The passenger service ceased here when the branch closed on 15th September 1958. This is the lower line on the left and freight continued on it until 1963. The Euston to Rugby line runs from right to left.

15.   A slip coach for Leamington Spa was tried for a short period around 1900. Many trains for the Leamington Spa single line originated at Northampton Castle, but a bay platform was created here in 1895 to facilitate branch operation. Both photographs were taken in about 1950, when the brick-built shelters on the up platform were still fairly new. (W.A.Camwell/SLS coll.)

─────── **For other views see *Bletchley to Rugby* pictures nos 97-100.** ───────

16.   There was a goods loop behind the fence on the up platform (right). No. 41227 rests by the water column upon arrival from Leamington Spa and No. 2 Box is in the distance. (W.A.Camwell/SLS coll.)

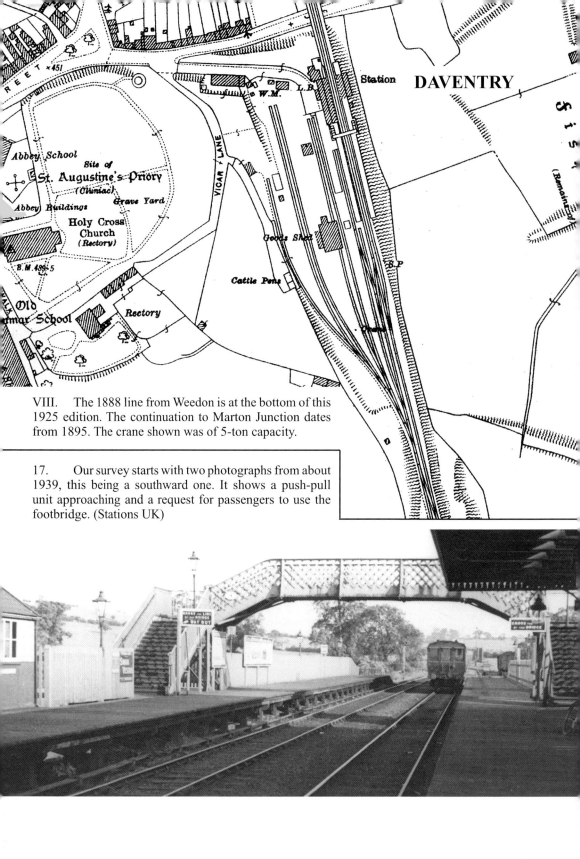

Station **DAVENTRY**

VIII.   The 1888 line from Weedon is at the bottom of this 1925 edition. The continuation to Marton Junction dates from 1895. The crane shown was of 5-ton capacity.

17.   Our survey starts with two photographs from about 1939, this being a southward one. It shows a push-pull unit approaching and a request for passengers to use the footbridge. (Stations UK)

18. The other end of the same train is seen. The signal box was in a hut on the right, behind the WAY OUT sign. (Stations UK)

19. The signalman raises the staff on 1st September 1958 as 2-6-2T no. 41228 approaches his boarded crossing on its way from Leamington Spa to Northampton Castle. Gas lighting prevails. (H.F.Wheeller/R.S.Carpenter coll.)

20.   The same train accelerates south and runs on the single line. The goods yard remained open until 2nd December 1963. The long headshunt is parallel to the train.
(H.F.Wheeller/R.S.Carpenter coll.)

21.   The photographer's Hillman 10 graces the exterior on 25th July 1959, by which time the building was used by just the goods clerk. The population rose from 3780 in 1901 to 6060 in 1961.
(H.C.Casserley)

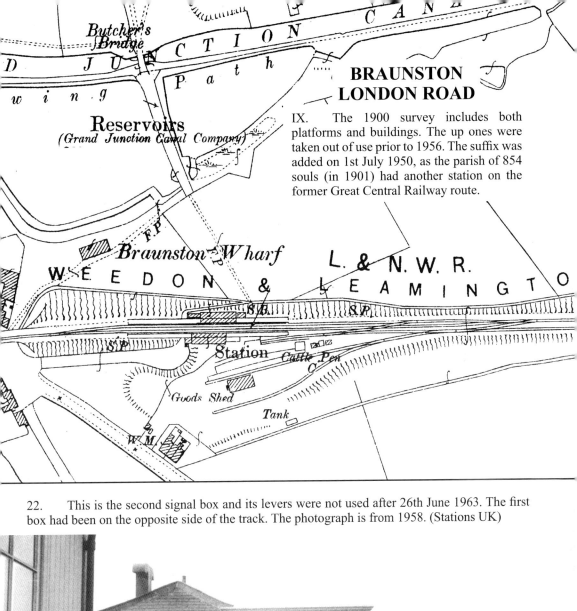

BRAUNSTON
LONDON ROAD

IX.   The 1900 survey includes both platforms and buildings. The up ones were taken out of use prior to 1956. The suffix was added on 1st July 1950, as the parish of 854 souls (in 1901) had another station on the former Great Central Railway route.

22.   This is the second signal box and its levers were not used after 26th June 1963. The first box had been on the opposite side of the track. The photograph is from 1958. (Stations UK)

23.   The goods shed is visible, but not the 5-ton crane listed in 1938. The signalling allowed the passing of a goods train only. The line left Northamptonshire west of the station and passed under the GCR. (B.W.L.Brooksbank)

FLECKNOE

X.   The 1905 edition reveals how two roads south of the crossroads were diverted to pass over the bridge; the arrangement persists today.

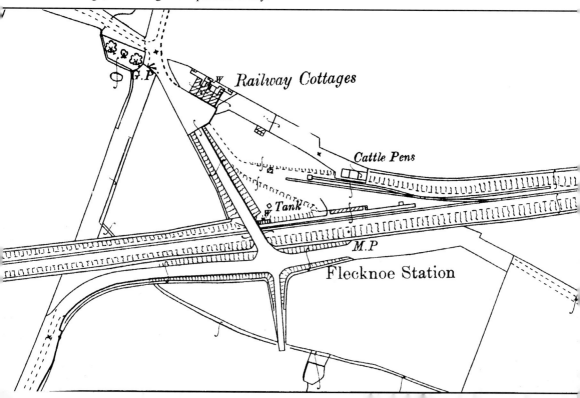

24.	The solitary member of staff was the subject for a postcard, but there was no-one between January 1917 and March 1919, as a wartime economy measure. The sectional building had been prefabricated at Crewe. (Lens of Sutton coll.)

25.	No passenger trains called after 3rd November 1952, but there was a part-time goods clerk until 1956. Freight traffic ceased on 2nd December 1963. The photograph was taken ten years earlier. (R.M.Casserley coll.)

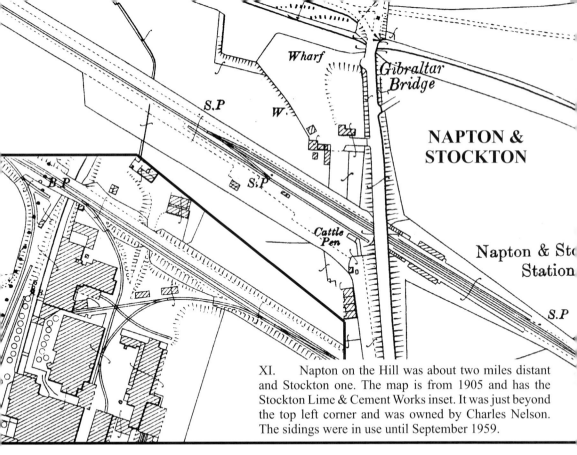

Wharf

Gibraltar
Bridge

S.P

W

**NAPTON &
STOCKTON**

S.P

B.P

Cattle
Pen

Napton & St
Station

S.P

XI.   Napton on the Hill was about two miles distant
and Stockton one. The map is from 1905 and has the
Stockton Lime & Cement Works inset. It was just beyond
the top left corner and was owned by Charles Nelson.
The sidings were in use until September 1959.

26.   The down platform has extensive floral decoration and the goods yard is apparently busy.
Stockton had a population of 877 in 1901. There were similar steps on the up platform. The lever
frame was situated behind the door where the man is standing. (Lens of Sutton coll.)

27.   Approaching is a train from Leamington Spa on the last day of passenger service, 13th September 1958. Stockton Cement Works is seen beyond the goods yard, which was in use until 2nd December 1963. (P.Kingston)

28.   The same train is seen from the bridge and waits for the signal to be cleared from the room behind the open door. The frame therein was in use until 25th June 1961. (P.Kingston)

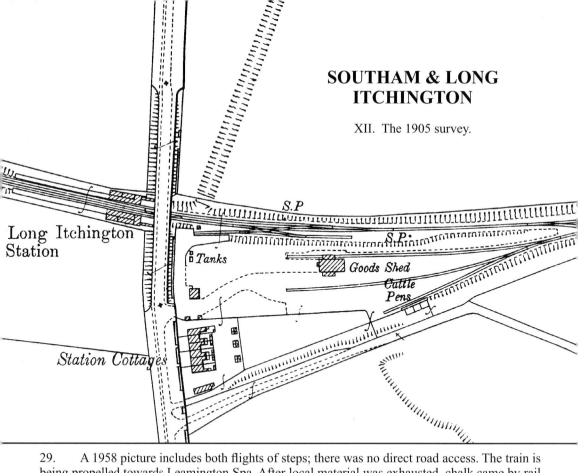

SOUTHAM & LONG ITCHINGTON

XII. The 1905 survey.

Long Itchington Station

S.P

S.P.

Tanks

Goods Shed

Cattle Pens

Station Cottages

29.   A 1958 picture includes both flights of steps; there was no direct road access. The train is being propelled towards Leamington Spa. After local material was exhausted, chalk came by rail for cement making from Totternhoe until 1965, when a pipeline was completed from Kemsworth, near Dunstable. The goods yard was open until 5th July of that year. Coal supplies continued until 1985, via Marton Junction. (Stations UK)

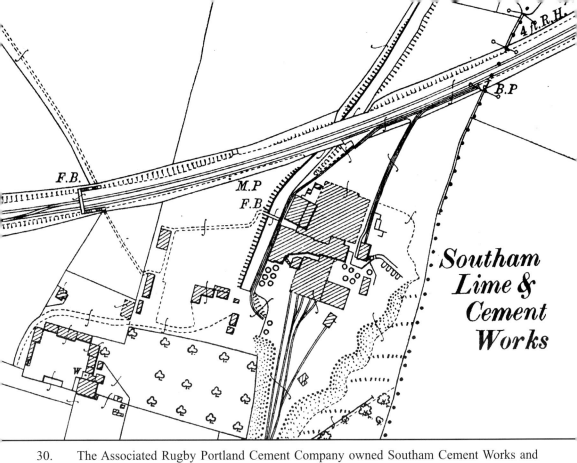

30.   The Associated Rugby Portland Cement Company owned Southam Cement Works and four of its Pecketts were recorded on 27th October 1956, shortly after its 1ft 11½ins gauge system had closed. From the left are *Triassic*, *Liassic*, *Mesozoic* and *Jurassic*. The works closed completely in 1999. (R.M.Casserley)

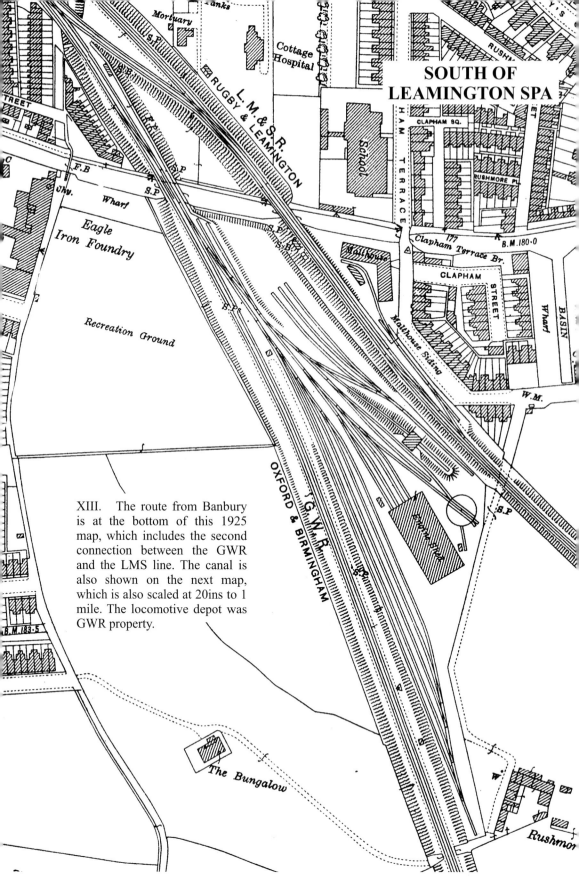

SOUTH OF
LEAMINGTON SPA

Mortuary

Cottage Hospital

School

CLAPHAM SQ.

RUSHMORE PL.

B.M.180.0

Clapham Terrace Br.

CLAPHAM

STREET

Wharf

BASIN

W.M.

L. M. & S. R.

RUGBY & LEAMINGTON

Malthouse

Malthouse Siding

S.P.

S.B.

F.B.

Wharf

Eagle
Iron Foundry

Recreation Ground

B.Ps.

Engine Shed

S.P.

OXFORD & BIRMINGHAM

G. W. R.

XIII. The route from Banbury
is at the bottom of this 1925
map, which includes the second
connection between the GWR
and the LMS line. The canal is
also shown on the next map,
which is also scaled at 20ins to 1
mile. The locomotive depot was
GWR property.

B.M.183.5

The Bungalow

Rushmor

Rushmo

31.   The name shown on this ex-LNWR box in 1958 was LEAMINGTON G W Jct. The signals on the left of this northward view are on the Paddington main line. The box closed on 24th June 1963. (P.Kingston)

December 1953

				Week Days only																					
Miles		a.m	a.m	a.m	a.m	a.m	a.m	a.m	a.m a.m a.m	p.m p.m p.m				p.m p.m		p.m p.m p.m		p.m p.m p.m	
	Northampton (Castle)... dep	6 55 7 10	..	..	8 15	..	..	8 45	.. 8 55 9 52 10 5	..	12 17 1 35	..		..	2 32	..	..	5 15	..	6 14	..	..	7 12 9 35 10 0	..
4¾	Blisworth... { arr / dep	7 .. 7 20	..	..	8 25	..	..	8 5F	.. 9 F 10 2 10 15	..	12 27 1 45	Saturdays only	..	..	2 45	..	..	5 25	..	6 24	..	..	7 22 9 45 10 10	..
11½	Weedon............		Except Saturdays	..	..	9 0	..	..		..	..	2 12		..	..	..	..	6 30		..			Saturdays only
15¾	Daventry { arr / dep			..	9 9 / 9 13	..	..		..	..	2 21 / 2 24		..	..	..	..	6 46 / 6 55		..			
19	Braunston			..	9 21	..	..		..	..	2 32		..	..	..	..	7 14		..			
25	Napton and Stockton......		8 12	..	9 33	..	..		..	..	2 45		..	4 55	..	..	7 21		..			
27	Southam & Long Itchington		8 18	..	9 39	..	..		..	..	2 K59		..	5 0	..	..	7 33		..			
34¾	Leamington Spa Avenue		8 35	..	9 56	..	..		..	..	3 16		..	5 20	..	..	7 39		..			
35	Leamington Spa A ... arr		8 40	..	10 0	..	..		..	..	3 59		..	5 50	..	..	7 56 / 8 15		..			

				Week Days only																	
Miles		a.m a.m	a.m	a.m	a.m	a.m	p.m	p.m	p.m	p.m p.m p.m		p.m		p.m	p.m		p.m
	Leamington Spa A......	7-10	..	..	..	..	12 50		..	2 37 / 4 8	..	..	..	..	..	6 10	..
¼	Leamington Spa Avenue	7 16	7 30	..	..	..	12 55	Saturdays only	..	2 43 / 4 20	..	..	..	..	..	6 30	..
8	Southam & Long Itchington	7 31	7 45	..	..	..	1 10		..	2 58 / 4 35	..	..	..	..	..	6 45	..
10	Napton and Stockton......	7 37	7 51	..	..	..	1 17		..	3 4 / 4 41	..	..	..	..	..	6 51	..
16	Braunston............	7 50	8	..	..	..	1 30		..	3 17	..	..	..	..	..		..
19½	Daventry { arr / dep	7 58 / 8 0	..	..	..	..	1 38 / 1 42		..	3 25 / 3 27	..	..	..	..	..		..
23¾	Weedon............	8 8	..	..	..	..	1 50		..	3 35	..	..	..	..	..		..
30¾	Blisworth... { arr / dep	6 54	..	..	8 42 / 9 20	..	10 20 / 12 40		2 5 / 3 54 0	3 47	..	5 32 / 7 35	..	..	10 5 / ..		
35	Northampton (Castle). arr	7 5	..	..	8 52 / 9 30	..	10 30 / 12 51		2 15 / 3 15 4 11		..	5 43 / 7 45	..	..	10 15		

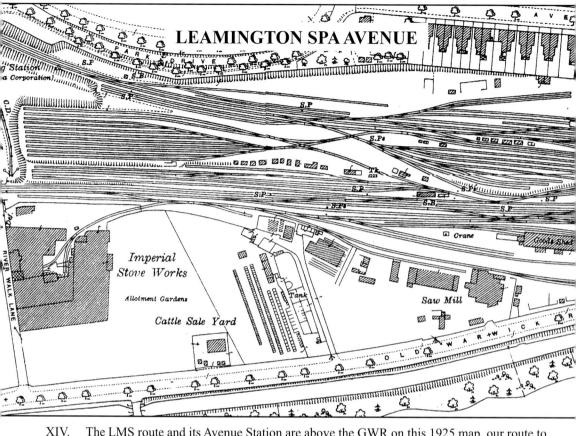

LEAMINGTON SPA AVENUE

Imperial Stove Works

Allotment Gardens

Cattle Sale Yard

Tank

Saw Mill

Crane

XIV.   The LMS route and its Avenue Station are above the GWR on this 1925 map, our route to Kenilworth being top left. The single line link between the two routes (right) came into use on 26th January 1864; a double track replacement was opened on 10th July 1908. It was beyond the right border of the map and faced the opposite direction. A new link was provided on 27th May 1966, west of the station. Beyond the right border was originally a wooden lattice bridge over the High Street. At 139ft 9ins, it was the longest in the UK when built. There were also 60 brick arches.

32.   A poor postcard indicates the generous accommodation provided at this important location. The terms "Spa" and "Avenue" were applied from 1913, but not "Royal", although the town uses it. (Lens of Sutton coll.)

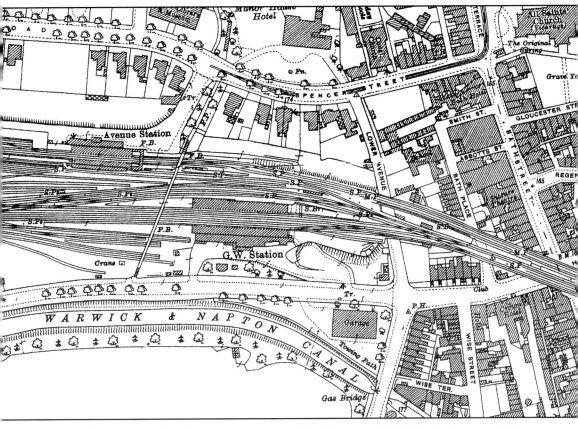

33.   Waiting to depart for Coventry sometime in 1937 is 0-6-0 no. 3329. Part of the bay platform and GWR station can be seen on the right. (G.Coltas/M.J.Stretton coll.)

34.　Whilst the GWR station opened in 1852, its neighbour (illustrated), dates from February 1854. Leaving from it on 16th August 1947 is 2-4-2T no. 6669, bound for Weedon and Northampton Castle. Behind is 2-6-2T no. 204. (W.A.Camwell/SLS coll.)

35.　It is 13th September 1958 and we witness one of the last trains to Weedon. We can also enjoy the exceptional woodwork visible on some of the station buildings, although the fine valance has gone. (P.Kingston)

36.   West of the platforms was Leamington Spa box, which served the ex-LNWR lines and closed on 15th May 1966. There were 51 levers in its frame. The starting signal on the left is for the bay platform and is seen in 1959. (P.Kingston)

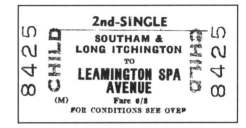

37.   Recorded on 29th April 1961 are the two sidings to the end-loading dock and a DMU bound for Nuneaton Trent Valley, via Coventry. (P.Kingston)

The GWR engine shed and station can be seen in pictures 32 to 42 in our *Banbury to Birmingham* album.

38.   The date is 29th April 1962 and no. D310 has been diverted with a Wolverhampton to Euston express, but it is not stopping here. The station closed on 18th January 1965 and was demolished in 1977. Goods traffic ceased on 4th April 1966, but coal came in for some time after this. (P.Kingston)

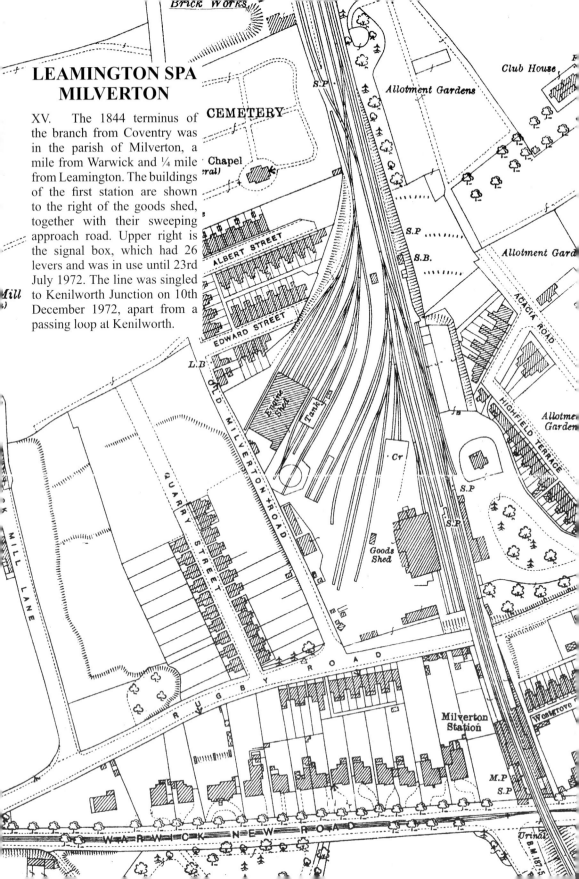

LEAMINGTON SPA MILVERTON

CEMETERY

XV. The 1844 terminus of the branch from Coventry was in the parish of Milverton, a mile from Warwick and ¼ mile from Leamington. The buildings of the first station are shown to the right of the goods shed, together with their sweeping approach road. Upper right is the signal box, which had 26 levers and was in use until 23rd July 1972. The line was singled to Kenilworth Junction on 10th December 1972, apart from a passing loop at Kenilworth.

Brick Works

Club House

Allotment Gardens

S.P.

Chapel
ral)

S.P.

S.B.

Allotment Gard

Mill
)

ALBERT STREET

EDWARD STREET

ACACIA ROAD

L.B.

OLD MILVERTON ROAD

Allotme
Garden

Engine
Shed

Tank

HIGHFIELD TERRACE

MILL LANE

QUARRY STREET

Cr

S.P.

S.P.

Goods
Shed

RUGBY ROAD

Milverton
Station

Westgrove

M.P.
S.P.

WARWICK NEW ROAD

Urinal

B.M.187.5

39. The second station was opened on 2nd March 1884, when the route northwards was doubled to Kenilworth Junction and the Berkswell Loop came into use for freight. Direct trains to Birmingham, avoiding Coventry, began on 2nd June following. (Lens of Sutton coll.)

40. The first engine shed was in use from 1844 until 1881. The second locomotive depot opened in 1884 and was closed on 17th November 1958. It is seen through smoke in September 1958 and was usually known as Warwick Depot. (P.Kingston)

41.   In cleaner air on the same day, we find 0-6-0 no. 44395 on the vacuum operated 57ft turntable, adjacent to Milverton Road. The chimney on the left is for the sand drier. (P.Kingston)

42.   The code was 8W, a sub-shed of Rugby, but 8E was also a LMS code; BR (LMR) used 2C. Some of the six roads are seen on 18th November 1958. (P.Kingston)

43.   The station was named Leamington initially, Milverton for Warwick in 1854, Warwick in 1856 and in 1857 it was renamed Warwick (Milverton). Then Leamington (Milverton) in 1860, Leamington Milverton (Warwick) in 1876, Warwick (Milverton) in 1884, until it became Leamington Spa Milverton in 1952. A Coventry-Leamington Spa Avenue service stands at the wooden platform in 1958. (P.Kingston)

LONDON, RUGBY, COVENTRY, LEAMINGTON SPA WARWICK, and BIRMINGHAM

Week Days

(Railway timetable, November 1941)

References:
A Arr. 8 10 aft.
Aa Calls at 7 36 aft. to set down only.
B Night time.
R Station for Yardley 1¼ miles.
C New Street.
E or E Except Saturdays.
J Sunday night.
Restaurant Car.
S or S Saturdays only.
Through Carriage.
Third class only

November 1941

44. No. 41228 is near the end of its journey to Leamington Spa Avenue in June 1959. Fire buckets are ready on both platforms. Only the street level booking office was brick-built. (P.Kingston)

45. A diverted Euston to Liverpool express passes the goods yard, which closed on 11th November 1963. The original station up platform is in the left distance as no. 44863 runs by on 13th June 1959. The yard had a 7-ton crane in 1938. (P.Kingston)

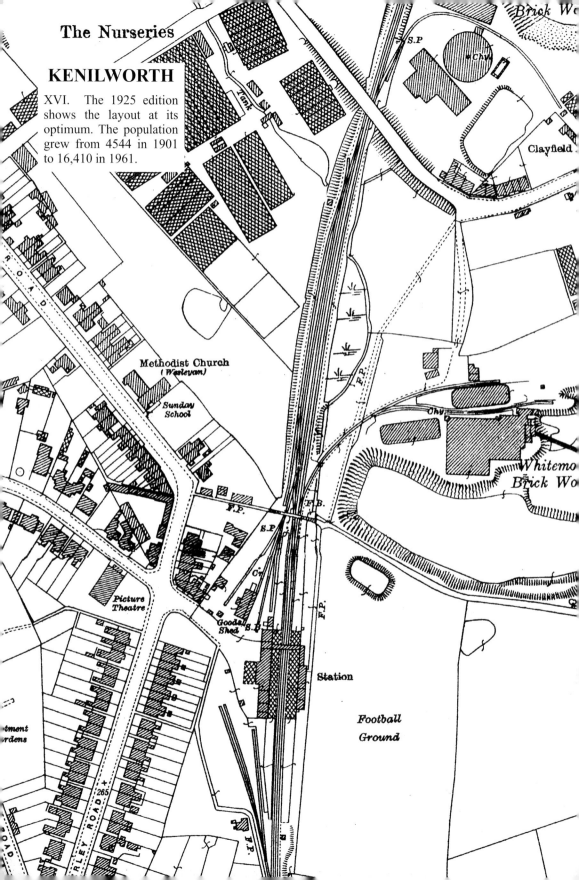

The Nurseries

KENILWORTH

XVI. The 1925 edition shows the layout at its optimum. The population grew from 4544 in 1901 to 16,410 in 1961.

Brick Wo

S.P

Chy

Clayfield

Tank

Methodist Church
(Wesleyan)

Sunday School

F.P.

Chy

Whitemo
Brick Wo

F.P.

F.B.

S.P.

C.

Picture Theatre

F.P.

Goods Shed S.B.

Station

Football Ground

tment rdens

RLEY ROAD

265

ROAD

ROAD

46.   A train of four-wheelers is northbound in this postcard view from around 1910. The town had an historic market, which still exists. (Lens of Sutton coll.)

47.   Southbound in low evening sunshine is no. 3704 on 25th August 1936, while shunting proceeds near the second footbridge. (G.Coltas/R.M.Casserley coll.)

48. The public footbridge was the vantage point for this record of 2-4-2T no. 6754, bound for Coventry in 1938. (G.Coltas/M.J.Stretton coll.)

49. The west elevation was probably photographed just after the war, as the canopy glass is all missing and LMS poster boards are evident. (R.M.Casserley coll.)

50.   On the right is the 30-lever signal box, which functioned until 7th January 1968. The photograph was taken about ten years earlier. The goods yard closed on 4th January 1965. The last regular coal traffic on the line was from Coventry Colliery to Didcot Power Station in 1991. Passenger service was withdrawn on 18th January 1965 and the station was demolished in 1969. Regular long distance passenger trains used the route again from 2nd May 1977. (Lens of Sutton coll.)

NORTH OF KENILWORTH

51.   Kenilworth Junction is seen in about 1950 as a diverted train takes the curve to the direct line to Berkswell. On the right is the route to Coventry, which had been single, but, in March 1916, a passing loop and signal box was provided at Gibbet Hill. It had 30 levers. (Both boxes closed on 10th December 1972.) The section north of here to Coventry was double from 29th August 2007. The last regular train over the Berkswell Loop was the 5.9pm (SX) from Birmingham New Street on 3rd July 1959. Freight continued until 17th January 1969. We now travel the main line. (H.F.Wheeller/R.S.Carpenter coll.)

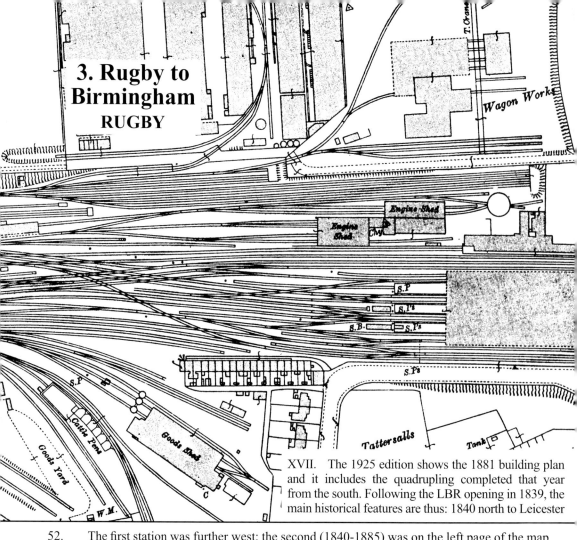

3. Rugby to Birmingham
RUGBY

Wagon Works

Engine Shed *Chy*

Engine Shed

S.P

S.P's

S.B. *S.P's*

S.P's

S.P.

Cattle Pens

Goods Yard

Goods Shed

C

W.M.

Tattersalls *Tank*

XVII. The 1925 edition shows the 1881 building plan and it includes the quadrupling completed that year from the south. Following the LBR opening in 1839, the main historical features are thus: 1840 north to Leicester

52. The first station was further west; the second (1840-1885) was on the left page of the map and this was the entrance to it. The third suffered intermittent surgery in 1941-2008, culminating with the provision of two new through platforms. (A.Dudman coll.)

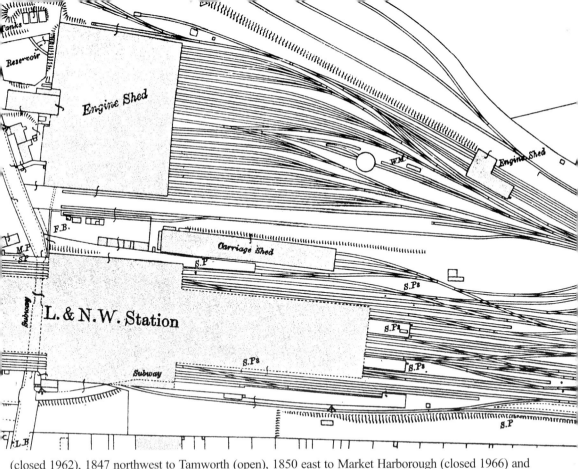

(closed 1962), 1847 northwest to Tamworth (open), 1850 east to Market Harborough (closed 1966) and 1851 southwest to Leamington Spa (closed 1959). The Leicester route was Midland Railway in 1844-1923; its engine sheds and adjacent small station are on the left page. Only part of the LNWR locomotive and engineering complex is shown on the right one. Its goods depot (1881-1965) is lower left.

53.　　The map indicates the great extent of the roofing and this postcard shows the down through platform, the subway entrance and a Webb compound 2-2-2-0 with an arrival from London, bound for Birmingham. (LNWR/P.Q.Treloar coll.)

54.   This is from almost the same viewpoint in 1961 and records the effect of the wartime loss of glass and subsequent patchwork. The signal box is No. 2 and the freight train is on the down through part of the scissors crossover. This allowed two trains to occupy the platform simultaneously. (Stations UK)

55.   At the west end of the station on 15th August 1962 is 4-6-0 no. 45684 with freight; the DMU is in the bay platform numbered 6. The term MIDLAND on the board was applied from 1948 until 1970. (P.Kingston)

56.   The same platforms are seen in the other direction on 29th November 1984, as class 310 EMU departs for Birmingham and puddles dry out under the defective roof. Installation of colour light signals was completed on 14th September 1964. All four northern bays were taken out of use at about that time. (J.C.Gillham)

57.   The entrance was transformed to a modern style and is seen in September 1992. An electrification gantry penetrates the old roof in an incompatible manner. (D.A.Thompson)

58.   This is the top of the subway seen in picture 53 and some brick buildings which have survived from the 1880s, in a changed ambiance. Reroofing began in 1992 as part of a lengthy upgrading and some of which is seen in 2007. (V.Mitchell)

59.   The entrance was undergoing a drastic rebuild and is pictured on 7th May 2007. It would give the convenience of a ticket office at road level and not on the platform. A new platform 1 was made available for the down fast line on 29th May 2007. As a result, existing No. 1 became 2 and No. 2 became 4. The new nos 5 and 6 came into use on 27th August 2008. (V.Mitchell)

WEST OF RUGBY

60.   Reference to map III will show that the route to Coventry is almost straight and that there was only one intermediate station. Up trains were provided with a flyover west of Rugby from 17th September 1962. Earlier, Holbrook Park water troughs had been available about two miles from the station. "Prince of Wales" class 4-6-0 no. 252 is heading the up "Irishman Express" and takes water in about 1923. Officially known as Church Lawford, the troughs were taken out of use in March 1965. (R.S.Carpenter coll.)

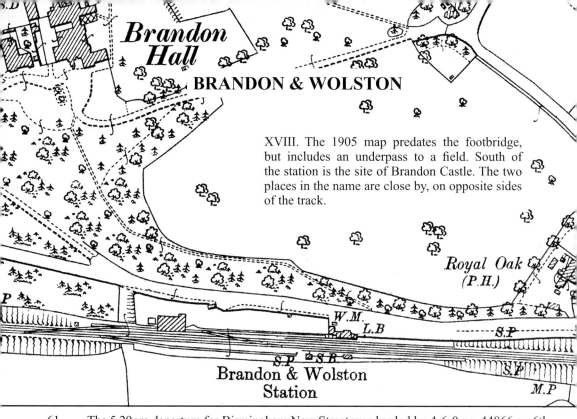

Brandon Hall

BRANDON & WOLSTON

XVIII. The 1905 map predates the footbridge, but includes an underpass to a field. South of the station is the site of Brandon Castle. The two places in the name are close by, on opposite sides of the track.

Royal Oak (P.H.)

P

W.M.

L.B

S.P

S.P S.B

S.P

M.P

Brandon & Wolston Station

61.   The 5.29pm departure for Birmingham New Street was hauled by 4-6-0 no. 44866 on 6th May 1960. The down refuge siding is in the foreground. The box had an 18-lever frame, which lasted in use until 13th September 1964. (D.A.Johnson)

62.   The 6.29pm to Rugby was recorded on 15th August 1960 behind 2-6-4T no. 42267. Binley Colliery sidings were 1½ miles further west and Brandon Ballast Pit signal box, which had 32 levers, controlled them. The box closed on 1st March 1964. (D.A.Johnson)

63.   The station closed to passengers on 12th September 1960, was photographed on 3rd September 1962 and closed to freight on 7th December 1964. Visible is the 3-ton crane and also the signalman, plus his motor cycle. (B.W.L.Brooksbank)

64.   No. 46137 *Prince of Wales Volunteers South Lancashire* races towards Rugby on 30th May 1959 and passes Humber Road Junction box. This controlled access to the Avoiding Line from Nuneaton, which bypassed Coventry. It opened on 10th August 1914. The southern part closed in November 1963 and the box followed on 13th September 1964. It was known as Pinley Junction from 4th May 1913 until 26th July 1914. (P.Glenn/R.S.Carpenter coll.)

65.　　　Whitley Wharf was a public goods depot and is seen in this May 1959 eastward view from the A4114 bridge, which is on the outskirts of Coventry. The box became a ground frame on 15th April 1962 and closed on 29th June 1966. (H.F.Wheeller/R.S.Carpenter coll.)

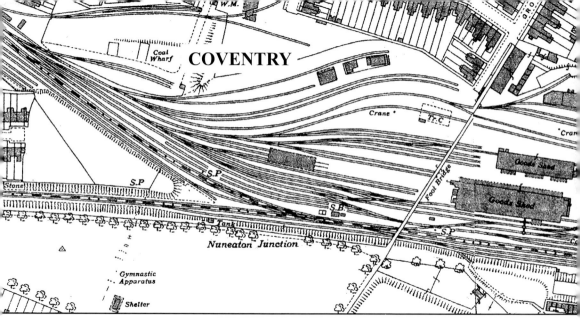

XIX.   Our route is from right to left and the Kenilworth to Nuneaton line is from bottom to top. The travelling crane (Tr.C) could lift 25 tons. The map is from 1937 and is at 20ins to 1 mile.

66.   The entrance was on the north side of the station, but there was also an access ramp on the down side. Unlike much of the city, the station was not destroyed by Nazi bombing. There were two slip coaches off expresses from Euston from February 1914 for a short while.
(Lens of Sutton coll.)

67.   The shed came secondhand from Crewe in 1897 and was larger than the first one of 1866. It is on the right of the map and was photographed in July 1936. The shed code was then 2F and it became 2D in 1948. (W.A.Camwell/SLS coll.)

68.   Looking towards Birmingham on 5th October 1957, we see 4-6-0 no. 44823, the roof of the ramp, the luggage lift and the former MR engine shed. It was in use from 1865 until 1904. The MR and LNWR ran a joint service between Nottingham and Leamington Spa Avenue for a few years from 1910. (H.F.Wheeller/R.S.Carpenter)

69.   The ex-LNWR engine shed received a new roof in 1957, but was closed on 17th November 1958. It is seen six months earlier, with No. 1 Box in the background. Its 52 levers were taken out of use on 15th April 1962. (H.C.Casserley)

70.   Reconstruction work had started when Cravens class 129 parcels car no. M55998 was photographed in 1959. Through lines would soon become history and all would have platforms. (P.Kingston)

71.   It is 6th May 1960 and the new footbridge is complete behind the old one. Blowing off is 2-6-4T no. 40157 and alongside it is no. 40207 with a DMU behind it. This eastward view has No. 1 box in the distance. (D.A.Johnson)

72.   The new station is rising in the background as we view the goods yard on 3rd September 1960. On the up main line is 2-6-0 no. 46445. (H.F.Wheeller/R.S.Carpenter coll.)

73.   The new power box functioned from 16th April 1962 and semaphore signals vanished. The new station was officially opened on 1st May 1962, about the time of this official photograph. Platform 1 would take 19 coaches, 2 and 3: 17, and 4: 13. (LMR/M.J.Stretton coll.)

8564
L. M. & S. R.
FOR CONDITIONS SEE NOTICES
BERKSWELL & B.C. TO
RUGBY(L.M.S.)
THIRD CLASS]   128 (S RUGBY   FARE 2/8 C
8564

London & North Western Ry.
Issued subject to the conditions & regulations in the Coy Time Tables Books Bills & Notices.
COVENTRY TO
MARSTON GREEN
THIRD CLASS]   120(S,)   [Parly
MARSTON GREEN   FARE 1/-
5176

74.   The great length of the stark new structure is clear in this record of the north and west elevations in 1977. It has been listed as Grade II, although some might like to read Grade 11 (eleven). A direct service to Nuneaton was restored in May 1987. (D.A.Thompson)

75.   The power signal box is in the background as no. 50031 takes the curve to Leamington Spa with the 13.45 Birmingham New Street to Paddington on 12th May 1990. The overhead wiring ends on the curve. The box closed on 29th August 2007, when control moved to the West Midlands Signalling Centre at Saltley. (D.A.Johnson)

CANLEY

76.   Situated in the suburbs of Coventry, transport for essential war workers was provided
here from 30th September 1940. The term HALT was applied until 6th May 1968. Both platforms
would take eight coaches. (Stations UK)

77.   "The Midlander" speeds west behind no. 45734 *Meteor* on 10th April 1954. The level
crossing is under the second coach. (P.Glenn/R.S.Carpenter coll.)

78. Seen from the footbridge on 19th July 1953 is a Sunday diversion, hauled by 4-6-0 no. 44937. The box had 15 levers and controlled only barriers after 3rd July 1966. (P.Glenn/R.S.Carpenter coll.)

79. Seen on 2nd May 1989, the barriers were worked remotely under CCTV after 4th November 1979. The level crossing was finally abolished on 14th June 2004. The original booking office and platform shelters were replaced in 1995. (D.A.Thompson)

TILE HILL

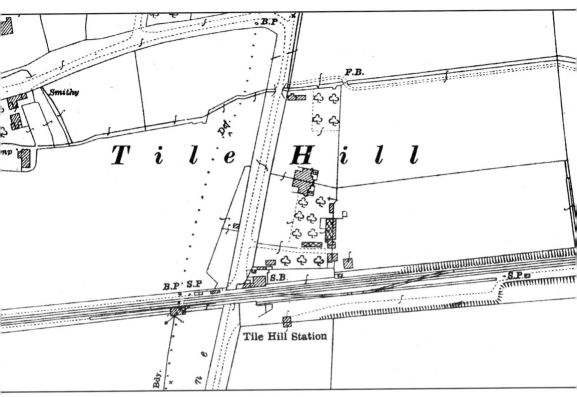

Smithy

T i l e   H i l l

B.P

F.B.

B.P S.P

S.B.

S.P

Tile Hill Station

Bdy.

XX.   The 1925 map shows rural environs, but the district is now part of the outer suburbs of Coventry. The station was opened by May 1848 and was known as Allesley Gate initially.

80.   A northward panorama in the early 20th century includes the entrance to the goods yard on the right and wicket gates for pedestrians on the left. (Lens of Sutton coll.)

81.   A 1964 westward view confirms that the platforms were still staggered. A new up one was opened on 15th August 1966 to eliminate this feature. The cattle pens and weigh house still stand, although the goods yard had closed. The signal box closed on 3rd July 1966. It was replaced by a 10-lever shunt frame which was used until 1st July 1979, when CCTV was also introduced. A down loop was still in place west of the station in 2008; it opened on 3rd May 1964. (Stations UK)

82.   Looking east on 2nd May 1989, we note that there were more than three parked cars and that the platforms matched. Both could take four coaches. The level crossing was eliminated on 20th September 2004 and a new road bridge came into use on 16th March 2005. A new building had been provided by that time. Beechwood Tunnel (300yds) is west of the station. (D.A.Thompson)

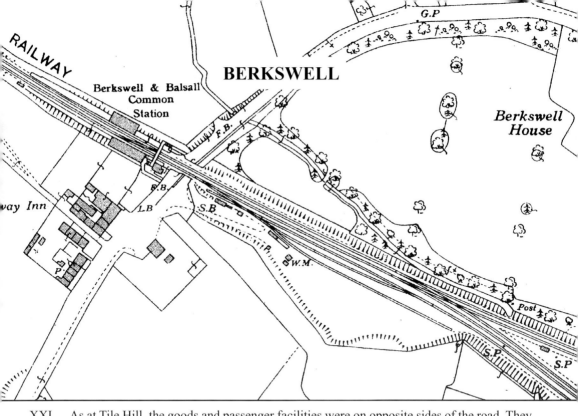

BERKSWELL

RAILWAY

Berkswell & Balsall Common Station

F.B.

G.B.

LB

S.B.

W.M.

ay Inn

P.

G.P

Berkswell House

Post

S.P.

S.P.

XXI.   As at Tile Hill, the goods and passenger facilities were on opposite sides of the road. They are shown on the 1937 edition, with the Kenilworth line lower right.

83.   The first station appears in print on 12th December 1844 and it had staggered platforms until about 1900. It was known as Dockers Lane until 1853. Much building work was undertaken in 1911. (SLS coll.)

84.   When the up platform was repositioned, a footbridge was provided to supplement the wicket gates. The suffix "& Balsall Common" was used from 1st February 1928.
(Lens of Sutton coll.)

85.   An eastward panorama from about 1950 includes Berkswell Loop curving right towards Kenilworth; a short siding near its route could still be seen in 2008. The signal box has a gate wheel and functioned with a 30-lever frame until 3rd July 1966. It controlled full lifting barriers until October 1979. There is an underpass adjacent to the level crossing. (R.S.Carpenter)

86.   Signalled for Coventry is 2-6-4T no. 42267 with a stopping train in around 1950. The local population was then still under 2000. The goods yard was closed on 4th January 1965. (R.S.Carpenter)

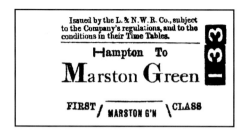

Issued by the L. & N.W.R. Co., subject to the Company's regulations, and to the conditions in their Time Tables.

Hampton   To

Marston Green

133

FIRST / MARSTON G'N \ CLASS

1 | 2 | 3 | PULL | 4 | 5 | 6

L. M. & S. R.   Valid ONE HOUR

FOR CONDITIONS SEE BACK

HAMPTON-IN-ARDEN

Admit ONE to Platform charge 1d
This ticket must be given up on leaving Platform

7 | 8 | 9 | 10 | 11 | 12

30 AU .2

041

87.   Speeding through on 10th June 1983 is no. 86240 *Bishop Eric Treacy* with a Birmingham to Euston express. There was no trace of the earlier buildings on the platforms, but the house remained standing. (B.Robbins)

88.   A view from May 1989 includes an engineers siding and platforms for four coaches each. The level crossing was closed on 24th May 2004, in favour of a widened underpass. (D.A.Thompson)

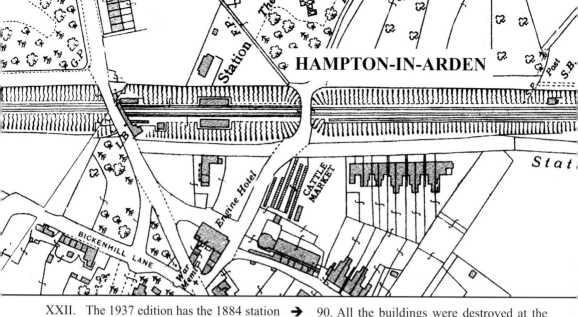

XXII. The 1937 edition has the 1884 station on the left page and the goods yard on the right one. The 5-ton crane is marked C. The first station is shown on the next map. The signal box (S.B.) had 22 levers and was worked until 3rd July 1966. The population was only 865 in 1901 and it rose to 1332 in 1961.

89.   This postcard features generous waiting rooms on both platforms and covered steps up to the booking office and station house. The suffix referred to the Forest of Arden and was added in 1876. (Lens of Sutton coll.)

→   90. All the buildings were destroyed at the time of electrification and a new ticket office was built. It can be seen top right. Twelve-coach platforms were provided in 1966, but the eastern ends were later fenced off. (D.A.Thompson)

↘   91. Another photograph from 1989 and this reveals that the replacement structure has tapered sides. The station was operated by InterCity until May 1976, by which time many passengers preferred to drive to the new Birmingham International, as long distance services were transferred there. (D.A.Thompson)

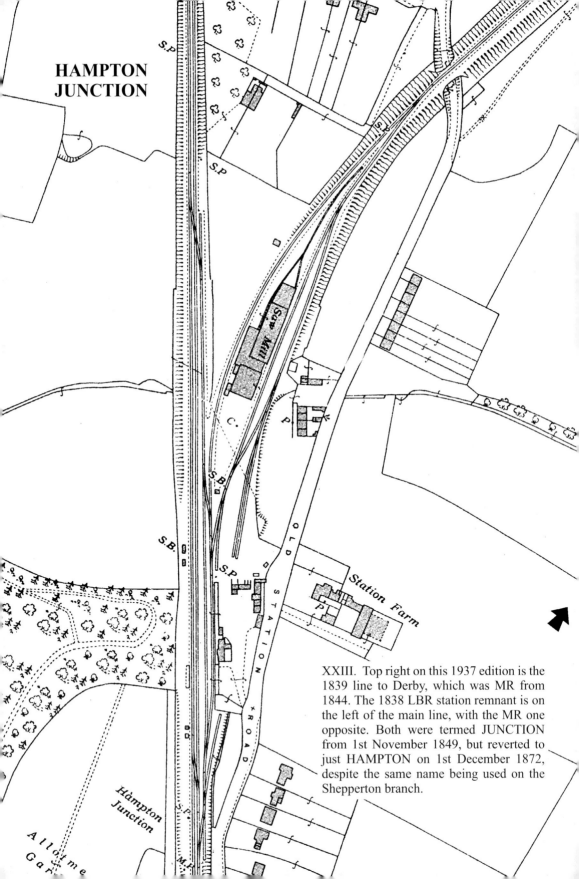

HAMPTON JUNCTION

S.P.

S.P.

Scrip Mill

C.

S.B.

S.B.

S.P.

P.

P.

Station Farm

O L D   S T A T I O N   R O A D

XXIII. Top right on this 1937 edition is the 1839 line to Derby, which was MR from 1844. The 1838 LBR station remnant is on the left of the main line, with the MR one opposite. Both were termed JUNCTION from 1st November 1849, but reverted to just HAMPTON on 1st December 1872, despite the same name being used on the Shepperton branch.

Hampton Junction

Allotme Gar

M.P.

S.P.

92.   The MR station is seen without its complete name. It ceased to have a passenger service after 1st January 1917, but some freight continued north until 1930. The remnant became a long siding until 4th January 1965, when the yard also closed. (W.A.Camwell/SLS coll.)

93.   The signal box is adjacent to the down main line and is seen in about 1962. It had 25 levers and functioned until 20th March 1966. Much of the area became a timber yard - hence the crane. The old building survives, being listed Grade II. (Lens of Sutton coll.)

BIRMINGHAM INTERNATIONAL

94.   The five-platformed station was opened on 26th January 1976 to serve the National Exhibition Centre and also the airport, which became Birmingham International in May 1984. The 10.37 Birmingham New Street to Euston was formed of BR Derby-built no. 310074 on 31st January 1987. (B.Morrison)

95.   The magnetic levitation principle was employed for transport of passengers between the station and airport (left). One of the two Maglev cabins is seen on 11th April 1990; they were the first in the world and ran from 7th August 1984 until 19th June 1995. They were replaced by buses until SkyRail began on 7th March 2003, using cable-worked cars. If you missed a trip by maglev, you can fly to Japan and levitate at 580 km/hr. (B.Morrison)

96. The roof suspension system for the NEC is evident as no. 86256 *Pebble Mill* propels the 15.19 Wolverhampton to Euston InterCity coaches on 26th April 1996. (B.I.Nathan)

97. All platforms were built for 15 coaches and on 6th August 2007 no. 4 was occupied by Pendolino no. 390003 *Virgin Hero*, bound for Euston. At no. 3 is Voyager no. 220026 *Stagecoach Voyager* forming the 07.30 Bournemouth to Edinburgh service. (B.Morrison)

98. Seen on the same day is Desiro class no. 350128 forming the 10.58 from Northampton to Birmingham New Street. These EMUs were built by Siemens with disc and regenerative braking in 2004-05. (B.Morrison)

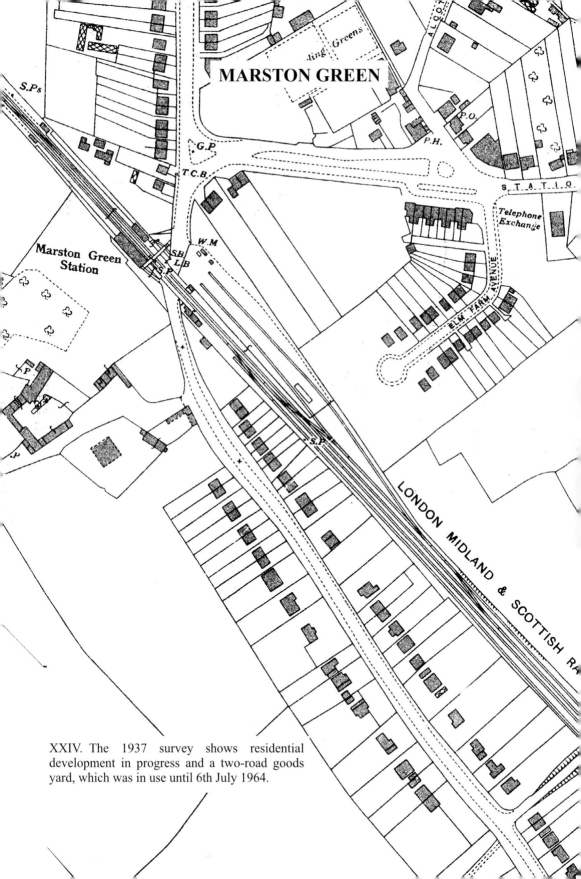

MARSTON GREEN

XXIV. The 1937 survey shows residential development in progress and a two-road goods yard, which was in use until 6th July 1964.

99.　　The first appearance in timetables was on 12th December 1844. The station is now on the edge of both the airport and Warwickshire. This eastward view is shortly before electrification and the loss of the classic canopies. The small signal box, near the gates, had 30 levers and was in full use until 3rd July 1966. It controlled only the crossing until closed in August 1976.
(Lens of Sutton coll.)

100.   Platforms were provided for eight coaches each and are seen just prior to closure of the signal box on 3rd July 1966. It had 30 levers and remained as a ground frame for a further ten years. (Lens of Sutton coll.)

101.   The 1984 building was recorded in 1989 showing the West Midlands Passenger Transport Authority's WM logo and brand name. Two brick-built shelters were provided on the platforms, plus an additional footbridge with ramps. (D.A.Thompson)

LEA HALL

102.   Two nine-coach platforms opened on 1st May 1939 to serve housing developments and they are seen in 1964 as electrification was at an early stage. (Stations UK)

103.   An eastward view on 22nd June 1971 includes both types of electric stock used for stopping services. They are class 310 (left) and 304. (D.A.Johnson)

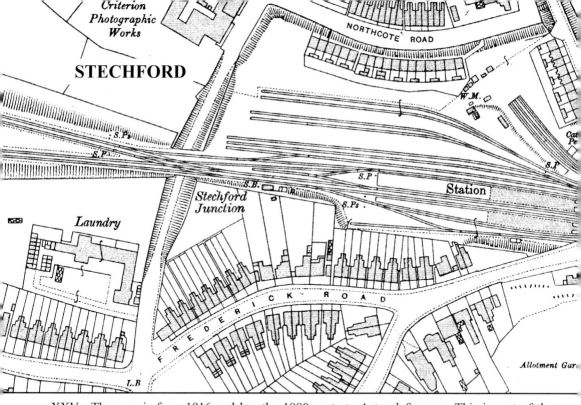

XXV. The map is from 1916 and has the 1880 route to Aston left upper. This is part of the alternative route to Wolverhampton, avoiding Birmingham.

104. The opening date estimate for the first station is as for Marston Green. This station was opened to the west of the original one on 1st February 1882. (R.M.Casserley coll.)

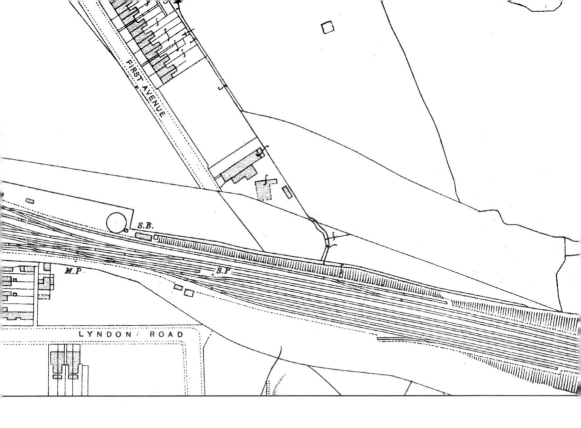

105.   This eastward panorama is from near the left border of the map in about the same period. The River Cole passes under the tracks just behind the camera. Stechford No. 2 Box is on the right. (Lens of Sutton coll.)

106.   The exterior was recorded in 1952 and destroyed by fire in April 1966. This was part of the 1882 development consequent to the station becoming a junction. (R.M.Casserley coll.)

107.   The wires are up, but demolition has not been completed and a gas light still stands. It is 1968. Three platform faces were with tracks in 2008, the up side having an island. They could take 6, 8 and 6 coaches. (Stations UK)

108.   No. 1 Box had 54 levers and No. 2 (picture 105) had 45; both closed on 3rd July 1966. The former was retained as a shunt frame and is seen on 6th February 1988 as a class 310 from Coventry passes. It has blue around the windows and yellow below. (B.Robbins)

109.   The ticket office was recorded on 2nd May 1989. Regular passenger trains on the Aston route ceased on 11th May 1990, when the Walsall service was withdrawn. But, most Marylebone to Wrexham trains used it from 28th April 2008, with one stop at Tame Bridge Parkway between Banbury and Telford. Wrexham & Shropshire was the open access operator, the service starting that day. (D.A.Thompson)

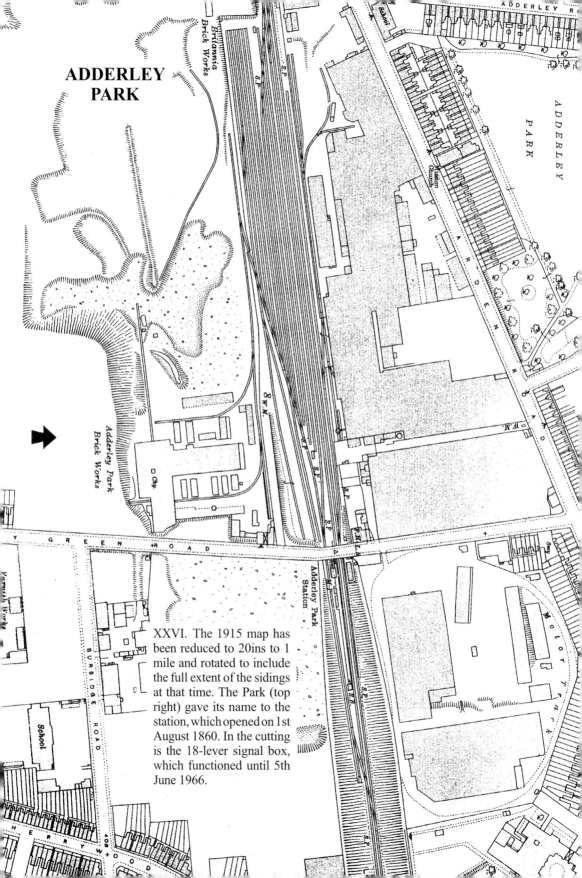

ADDERLEY PARK

XXVI. The 1915 map has been reduced to 20ins to 1 mile and rotated to include the full extent of the sidings at that time. The Park (top right) gave its name to the station, which opened on 1st August 1860. In the cutting is the 18-lever signal box, which functioned until 5th June 1966.

110.   An express bound for Euston accelerates east in about 1932. The small building on the left was still standing more than 70 years later. (R.S.Carpenter coll.)

111.   A westward panorama from the road bridge in October 1964 includes industrial, carriage and sorting sidings. Extreme left is the goods yard, which was in use until 1st March 1965. (R.J.Essery/R.S.Carpenter coll.)

112.   Hauled by no. 47401, a Paddington to Birmingham service passes through on 3rd June 1980. Each platform accommodates four cars. (T.Heavyside)

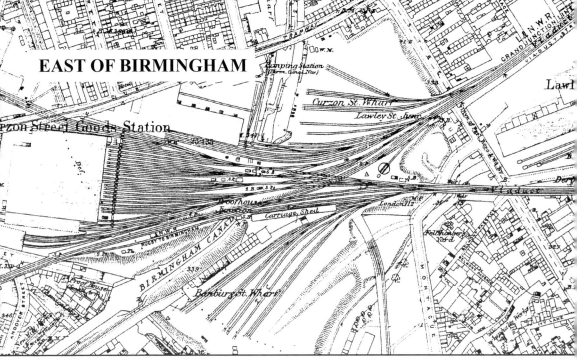

EAST OF BIRMINGHAM

XXVII. The line from Rugby (right) originally ran straight into the Curzon Street terminus (left), which is shown in use for goods on this 1890 edition at 20ins to 1 mile. Top right is the original route for trains to Manchester and Liverpool. Note the multitude of crossings. Lower left is the Proof House, after which the junction was named.

113.   Curzon Street station ceased to be used by passengers on 1st July 1854 and for goods on 23rd September 1968. The part shown on the map as offices had been a hotel at one period. The historic structure stood in uncomfortable isolation to be photographed from a passing train on 26th June 2008. (V.Mitchell)

BIRMINGHAM NEW STREET

XXVIII. The 1946 survey at 6ins to 1 mile has Adderley Park lower right and New Street lower left. Curzon Street is between the two. On the join of the pages is Lawley Street, which had been the terminus of trains from Derby in 1841-52. Until 1966-69, there were signal boxes at Exchange Sidings, Grand Junction and Proof House Junction.

114.　The nearest platforms were used by LNWR trains, while the southern ones served the MR. The former owned the station, but it was operated jointly from 1897. (Lens of Sutton coll.)

L. M. & S. R.
FOR CONDITIONS SEE BACK
MILITARY & NAVAL (FURLOUGH)
HAMPTON IN ARDEN TO
BIRMINGHAM (NEW STREET)
THIRD CLASS] 129(S)(MMF) FARE -/9N
BIRMINGHAM(N.ST)
223

2nd · SINGLE　　SINGLE · 2nd
Lea Hall to
Lea Hall　　　　　Lea Hall
Birmingham　　　　Birmingham
(New Street)　　　(New Street)
BIRMINGHAM (NEW STREET)
(M)　1/3　Fare　1/3　(M)
For conditions see over　For conditions see over
0333　0333

115.   A photograph from around 1900 gives a good impression of the extent of the glazed roof. This became a serious liability during the bombing in World War II and all the glass was lost. The 1885 steelwork had all gone by 1965. The locomotive is LNWR no. 3515 and it was in use from 1867 until 1907. (P.Q.Treloar coll.)

116.   Platform canopies had begun to appear in April 1948 and are seen on 29th July 1961, as a mixture of DMUs depart for Rugby during the brief diesel era on the route. However, there was still some steam operation. Part of the back of the Queens Hotel is included. (P.Kingston)

117.   An eastward panorama on 22nd April 1965 is from the ex-MR part of the station and includes part of the carriageway which had earlier run the length of the station and was termed Queens Drive. (B.W.L.Brooksbank)

Other albums including Birmingham stations are:
Birmingham to Wolverhampton,
Bromsgrove to Birmingham,
Worcester to Birmingham,
Banbury to Birmingham and
Stratford upon Avon to Birmingham.
New Street is in the first two, the middle two include Snow Hill and the last two Moor Street.

118.   No. 47189 is centre while no. 47543 stands with a Poole to Newcastle train on 15th August 1980. Mailbags and BRUTE trolleys help to recapture the age. (D.H.Mitchell)

119.   In contrast to the platform extremities, most of the rest has to be lit artificially at all times. The gloom has been constantly criticised. The low roof is evident in this photograph from May 1989. (D.A.Thompson)

120.   This was the station's only entrance in daylight and probably the most unimpressive in any city. Another was added at the west end, together with an extra footbridge, in 1992. (V.Mitchell)

121.   A panorama of the east end on 16th February 2008 includes the entrance just seen, in the centre. This is the hub of cross country and also local services, its success being reflected in the growth figures: about 250 trains per day in 1967, rising to 1350 in 2004. (V.Mitchell)

122.   The Wrexham service, mentioned in caption 109, ran non-stop through New Street twice on Mondays to Fridays, northbound only, and turned off the main line at Soho South Junction. The 10.17 from Marylebone passes through platform 7 at 12.24 on 30th June 2008, the three coaches and no. 67001 being hauled by no. 67017. Such are the bizarre consequences of open access operators competing with franchisees. (V.Mitchell)

Middleton Press

EVOLVING THE ULTIMATE RAIL ENCYCLOPEDIA

Easebourne Lane, Midhurst, West Sussex.
GU29 9AZ   Tel:01730 813169

www.middletonpress.co.uk   email:info@middletonpress.co.uk
A-978 0 906520   B- 978 1 873793   C- 978 1 901706   D-978 1 904474   E - 978 1 906008

OOP Out of print at time of printing - Please check availability   BROCHURE AVAILABLE SHOWING NEW TITLES